Facts About the Orangutan

By Lisa Strattin

© 2019 Lisa Strattin

FREE BOOK

FREE FOR ALL SUBSCRIBERS

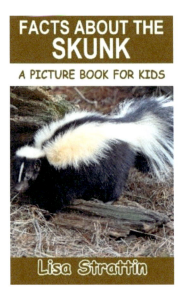

LisaStrattin.com/Subscribe-Here

BOX SET

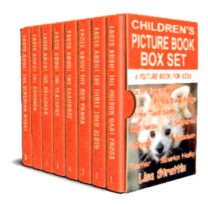

- **FACTS ABOUT THE POISON DART FROGS**
- **FACTS ABOUT THE THREE TOED SLOTH**
  - **FACTS ABOUT THE RED PANDA**
  - **FACTS ABOUT THE SEAHORSE**
  - **FACTS ABOUT THE PLATYPUS**
  - **FACTS ABOUT THE REINDEER**
  - **FACTS ABOUT THE PANTHER**
- **FACTS ABOUT THE SIBERIAN HUSKY**

LisaStrattin.com/BookBundle

Facts for Kids Picture Books by Lisa Strattin

Little Blue Penguin, Vol 92

Chipmunk, Vol 5

Frilled Lizard, Vol 39

Blue and Gold Macaw, Vol 13

Poison Dart Frogs, Vol 50

Blue Tarantula, Vol 115

African Elephants, Vol 8

Amur Leopard, Vol 89

Sabre Tooth Tiger, Vol 167

Baboon, Vol 174

Sign Up for New Release Emails Here

LisaStrattin.com/subscribe-here

All rights reserved. No part of this book may be reproduced by any means whatsoever without the written permission from the author, except brief portions quoted for purpose of review.

All information in this book has been carefully researched and checked for factual accuracy. However, the author and publisher makes no warranty, express or implied, that the information contained herein is appropriate for every individual, situation or purpose and assume no responsibility for errors or omissions. The reader assumes the risk and full responsibility for all actions, and the author will not be held responsible for any loss or damage, whether consequential, incidental, special or otherwise, that may result from the information presented in this book.

All images are free for use or purchased from stock photo sites or royalty free for commercial use.

Some coloring pages might be of the general species due to lack of available images.

I have relied on my own observations as well as many different sources for this book and I have done my best to check facts and give credit where it is due. In the event that any material is used without proper permission, please contact me so that the oversight can be corrected.

COVER IMAGE

By Eleifert - Own work, CC BY-SA 3.0, https://commons.wikimedia.org/w/index.php?curid=3913620

ADDITIONAL IMAGES

By David Arvidsson - originally posted to Flickr as DSC_1055_ApesEat, CC BY 2.0, https://commons.wikimedia.org/w/index.php?curid=7915499

By Nomo michael hoefner / http://www.zwo5.de - Own work, CC BY-SA 3.0, https://commons.wikimedia.org/w/index.php?curid=10616058

https://www.flickr.com/photos/verborrea/6250615799/

By I, Spolloman, CC BY-SA 3.0, https://commons.wikimedia.org/w/index.php?curid=2249833

By Postdlf, CC BY-SA 3.0, https://commons.wikimedia.org/w/index.php?curid=10627360

https://www.flickr.com/photos/12587661@N06/15850794791/

https://www.flickr.com/photos/12587661@N06/15850795831/

https://www.flickr.com/photos/hisgett/7109466297/

https://www.flickr.com/photos/baconizedhameister/8584547345/

https://www.flickr.com/photos/aoisakana/8947826791/

Contents

INTRODUCTION 9

CHARACTERISTICS 11

APPEARANCE 13

LIFE STAGES 15

LIFE SPAN 17

SIZE 19

HABITAT 21

DIET 23

ENEMIES 25

SUITABILITY AS PETS 27

INTRODUCTION

The Orangutan is one of the largest primates in the world and is the only member of the Great Ape family found outside of Africa. There are three species found in the steamy jungles on the islands of Borneo and Sumatra. These are the Bornean Orangutan, the Sumatran Orangutan and the Tapanuli Orangutan. The Bornean Orangutan is more numerous and widespread than its cousins on Sumatra with three distinct sub-species of Bornean Orangutan found in separate geographic regions on the island.

CHARACTERISTICS

Orangutans are solitary and that they spend almost all of their lives high up in the trees. Their large size means that it moves very slowly through the forest. They make nests to sleep in at night in the high canopy by folding branches over and padding them with leaves to make a bed for sleeping. Orangutans are not particularly territorial and will even tolerate feeding together around trees when an abundance of ripened fruits are available. Males will make their presence known by producing loud long-calls using their throat pouches to intimidate rival males and to attract a female on order to mate.

They are the largest tree-dwelling animal in the world, and also one of the most intelligent.

APPEARANCE

Orangutans have bright, red and orange hair which is why they are also called the Red Ape.

They are simply too heavy to leap like a monkey, so they use their long arms to swing on tree branches until they can get close enough to grab the next branch. Their hands and feet are both great at grasping onto branches and with their opposable thumbs, their digit (fingers) are very dexterous.

LIFE STAGES

After a gestation period that lasts for around nine months, the female gives birth to a single infant in a special nest she has built high in the trees. Young ones cling onto their mother's hair to stay safe and secure while she is moving through the trees searching for food and are not fully weaned until they are about three years old.

Young orangutans will stay with their mother until they are seven or eight years old. During this time, she teaches them the all of skills they need to survive in the forest. This includes learning about which plants to eat and where they can be found and teaching them how to use sticks and leaves as tools to make their life easier.

They don't breed until they are 12 to 15 years old.

LIFE SPAN

The average life span of an orangutan is 30 to 40 years. So, they enjoy a long life in the trees.

SIZE

Most adults are 4 to 5 feet tall and weigh from 90 to 200 pounds.

HABITAT

Although they would have once been found on a number of the forested islands in Indonesia, today they are only found on the islands of Borneo and Sumatra. They prefer the forests in lowlands where there is a plentiful and varied supply of food. They are also being found in hillside forests, in valleys and around peat-swamps, and there are a number of isolated populations on both of these islands in the mountain jungles at much higher altitudes.

All three species are considered threatened because of the decline of their habitats which have been deforested by humans for timber or cleared for agriculture.

DIET

Orangutans are omnivorous animals that eats a mixture of both plant and meat, but the majority of their diet is made up of the different types of fruit readily available in the trees where it lives. They spend most of their day eating, which may be the reason that they have evolved to being semi-solitary animals.

Despite the fact that they move throughout large ranges, they have their own patch of forest that is considered their home. This area is chosen due to there being enough food for them and their young.

They eat both ripe and unripe fruits including: mangoes, lychees, durian and figs which grow in abundance in some places where a number of individuals may meet up to feed together.

ENEMIES

Historically, the orangutans on both Borneo and Sumatra would have been threatened by a number of large, ground-dwelling carnivores. Large felines like tigers are the primary predators, as well as crocodiles and the occasional Asian Black Bear.

SUITABILITY AS PETS

There have been instances of people adopting Orangutans as pets in the illegal exotic pet trade, but this is a terrible idea. First, it would be very difficult to have a place large enough with tall trees for them to be happy and they are VERY BIG! You can probably see some of them in a suitable habitat at a zoo if you want to visit them.

COLOR ME

COLOR ME

COLOR ME

COLOR ME

COLOR ME

COLOR ME

COLOR ME

COLOR ME

COLOR ME

COLOR ME

Please leave me a review here:

LisaStrattin.com/Review-Vol-256

For more Kindle Downloads Visit Lisa Strattin Author Page on Amazon Author Central

amazon.com/author/lisastrattin

To see upcoming titles, visit my website at LisaStrattin.com– most books available on Kindle!

LisaStrattin.com

FREE BOOK

FOR ALL SUBSCRIBERS – SIGN UP NOW

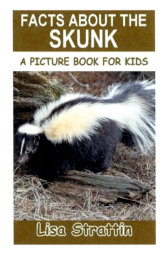

LisaStrattin.com/Subscribe-Here

LisaStrattin.com/Facebook

LisaStrattin.com/Youtube

Made in United States
Troutdale, OR
10/27/2023

14040111R00026